They're Just Boobs...
Get over it!

They're Just Boobs...
Get over it!

Boobs and the more important things in life

Tresa Lynn Bowlin

authorHOUSE®

AuthorHouse™
1663 Liberty Drive
Bloomington, IN 47403
www.authorhouse.com
Phone: 1-800-839-8640

Published by AuthorHouse   04/09/2013

ISBN: 978-1-4817-2682-5 (sc)
ISBN: 978-1-4817-2681-8 (e)

Library of Congress Control Number: 2013904479

About Women
But
Not for Women Only

We all have a common bond—Boobs

Women have boobs and
Men like Boobs

Contents

Note to Reader

Dear Reader:

This book does not include inappropriate material. You'll find nothing distasteful or immoral. The attraction of boobs has been clearly evident since they ever existed. The way I see it is, if boobs can be mentioned in the Bible, sure it is ok. So, lighten up a little as you read.

You'll be surprised to catch yourself laughing.

I hope you become more content with yourself. Who doesn't need that?!

Introduction

We all have stories or incidents in our lives that formed our opinions of how we look at each other and ourselves.

I want to share with you some of my stories of being a woman.

My opinions and random outbursts have always leaned on the comical side. (So I've been told).

I hope these paragraphs make you laugh or even cry because of something you remember from your past.

When you come to the end of this book, I want most of all for you to look at yourself and other women in a different way . . . and I hope when you look you find yourself smiling.

Ice Breaker: Mammogram or vice grip

We've heard all the warnings to protect our precious breast,

From wearing a good bra to doing monthly tests.

Advised to have a mammogram every single year.

Putting your boob in a vise grip almost brings a tear...

Place your boob upon a flat surface while a plastic plate smashes you flat...

It must have been a man who made this machine I am pretty sure of that!

How I Came to Write This Book (Maddie)

"Grandma, this is you! You're beautiful"

By Maddie (?) age 5

I started this book in my head over and over again but never put it on paper until Madeline came along.

Madeline (Maddie) is my first granddaughter and because of her curiosity and clever sayings, I decided this book was something I wanted to do.

I started babysitting Maddie when she was first born and when she turned four years old, I started writing.

Like most four year olds, Maddie was full of questions about boobs and other body parts.

She wanted to know why she didn't have boobs yet and when she could get some.

Now her parents are trying to instill values in her like modesty, so she understands body parts are private. Yet sometimes it takes kids a few times being told before they actually get it.

It always seemed so funny to me that this was something all kids noticed at a very early age.

Most families share the bathroom at one time or another. And kids are bugging mommy to come in the bathroom with her. (In my case-bugging grandma).

They always want to be in the room where you are changing or showering. Maddie would come in the room where I was changing and it didn't take long for the questions to start. Like "Grandma, why don't your boobs look like mommy's?" My interpretation was, of course, "Grandma's boobs are not youthful looking".

I tell Maddie everyday she is pretty and she is nice but that it is more important to be nice because looks change but attitude is long term.

I want her to be content with how she looks, no matter what.

Mostly, the reason for this book is to reinforce in all of us that there is more to you than your boobs . . . or your size or your hair color.

I want women to love their bodies. Even their boobs or the lack of boobs.

That's right women. We should love our boobs just as much men do. We need to fall in love with all of ourselves, not just the boobs.

Wardrobe Malfunction

My Grandma Beulah gave a whole new meaning to the words "wardrobe malfunction".

Beulah was my grandma on my dad's side and actually both of my grandmothers were big busted women. It is painfully clear that I did not inherit that gene.

As a kid, I would spend summers visiting my dad. He lived in Tennessee, which was very close to his parents, so I got to spend time with them also.

Grandma Beulah and Grandpa Elvie made summer fun. It was some of the best childhood memories I have. One incident with Grandma Beulah will forever be imbedded into my memory. It was the wardrobe malfunction that put all others to shame. Not only was I shocked and mortified for Grandma, I was more shocked to see that it didn't faze her at all.

This particular summer I was probably eleven years old. We were all getting ready for bed. Grandma came out of the bathroom from changing into her nightgown and she was clearly oblivious as to her appearance. She had one boob inside her nightgown and one on the outside. I still laugh when I think of it now, but at the time, I was mortified!

I never understood until I was older. I was embarrassed for her because there sat Grandpa Elvie. I knew Grandpa would be shocked but, much to my surprise, he was grinning from ear to ear. His face lit up like a Christmas tree.

I blurted out, "Grandma, put that back in there!" Never giving it a thought, Grandma picked up her 80 year old boob and dropped in back into her nightgown like she was flipping pancakes—just so matter of fact.

I was dumb founded at the time but now years later I realize that at any age men like to see boobs. Grandpa did anyway. As far as Grandma was concerned; she already knew they're just boobs.

Memory Lane

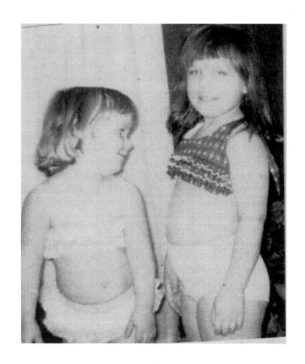

Let's travel back in time awhile.

Surely, ladies, you remember yourselves as little girls; when you started to develop and were so excited. You knew you were about to be the proud new owner of a bra.

Through the years, that excitement fizzles away and we actually come to loathe the contraption. For a short time though we are happy to be the recipient of the bra.

Now if you are a mother of daughters, you will get to revisit that excitement again when it's time for you to buy their first bra. If you have sons, you will see the excitement also. You just won't be shopping for a bra.

I am constantly reminded of when my kids were young and how the topic for boobs was not limited to just girls or adults. I remember when my daughter made her first request to go bra shopping. She was so pleased when she finally got one. I also remember when my son first noticed boobs . . . and basically,

11

that's all he talked about until he . . . well, got to see some.

It's funny to me how different the attitudes are from the mother's point of view versus the dad's. It's time to take your daughter shopping for her first bra. You happily escort the young lady into the girls' department. While you are browsing, dad is standing somewhere off to the side stricken with fear. He is on the verge of hyperventilating thinking that very soon some Neanderthal will be checking out his daughter the same way he has looked at other women. He starts to have a brief moment of remorse and recognizes the error of his ways.

We all know the remorse lasts for a short time, or, at least until the next time dad sees the neighbor lady washing the car in her bathing suit or goes for the newspaper in her pajamas.

But then again ladies . . . boys will be boys and they are just boobs.

Boys Will Be Boys

Of course boys will be boys. Is it human nature to look? I think it is. We would be lying if we as women said ourselves that we never look at or notice attractive men.

How can we expect men to have this super-human power to resist looking at a beautiful woman when we drop our jaw as Mr. Amazing walks by.

Now I understand there is a line that crosses over into disrespect.

I am not talking about that. There is a difference between noticing a pretty woman and being a womanizer. Simply put, men are creatures of vision and unless they walk around with blinders on their eyes . . . they will notice.

Let's get past that and look a little deeper. Look past the boobs . . . Deeper into her chest and there we discover her heart.

I truly believe most men, or at least the majority of them, know how to look at and love a woman. But let's face it girls, boys will be boys and just like my dad always said; "One look at boobs and a man turns into a blubbering idiot!"

Odd Insecurities

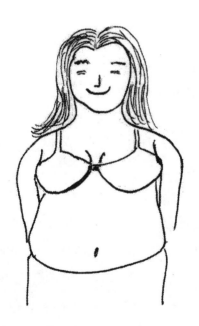

One thing I know for sure is that all women have these odd insecurities about themselves. From skinny girls to fat girls . . . even absolutely gorgeous girls doubt their beauty. They question what they look like to others and worse yet what they look like to themselves.

STOP THE DOUBTING! YOU ARE BEAUTIFUL!

We need not think men are never self-conscious either. We all face this senseless line of questioning.

"Does he think I am pretty?" "Does she think I am handsome?"

"Does he think I am fat?" "Does she think I am too short?"

Stop it! Look a little deeper. Look at what's really important within Yourself and lighten up on the other stuff. Beauty comes in so many forms. If we could really understand our worth we would know our value is something that cannot be measured. We would look at others differently and we would value what's beneath the skin more than what's on the surface. We would be confident and content and we would expect people to treat us accordingly.

One of the best dates I ever had was with this guy that had a weight problem. He had so much self-confidence, though, that I never noticed his size. He smiled all the time. He was a perfect gentleman and he made me laugh, so when he asked me out it was easy to say yes.

Did he question his appearance in his head? Maybe he did . . . but if he did, he never showed it. When our date was over he walked me to the door and kissed me goodnight. WOW! One of the best kissers ever!

That was something I would not have had if he or I let his size be important. We only dated a few times and even though there was not a love connection we have remained friends.

Since then he married a SKINNY beautiful girl who also looked past his size and saw what really mattered.

Confidence Speaks
Volumes

We don't want others to judge us by our looks yet most of us are never happy with what we look like either.

Big busted girls want a breast reduction.

Flat chested girls want an enlargement.

Short girls want to be petite.

Red-heads, blondes, brunettes . . . chubby or thin.

We have so many differences but are all the same within.

Sexy comes in all sorts of styles and people will not notice your flaws if you are content with yourself.

They will be drawn to your confidence. The most attractive think I have ever seen is a smile!

Double Standards

Society looks at others and makes opinions based on looks. It's not right, but it in fact happens. We have all done that right? Let's be honest. We have all been superficial at one time or another and we are always more critical of ourselves . . . men included. Although I do tend to think women are the recipients of a stricter double standard concerning appearance. If you don't believe it . . . think about this for a minute.

When people get married if the man gains a lot of weight they say "wow his wife must be cooking good for him". If the woman gains a lot weight the statement changes to "she really let herself go". If that isn't double standard I don't know what is.

I have to be honest I sometimes have a double standard mentality myself. I think when a man turns gray he looks distinguished. But when a woman turns gray she just looks older.

Sometimes we do get viewed or valued by our size or the shape of our bodies. That is not the way it is supposed to be.

We all need to reprogram our thinking. Myself included.

Open your mind and jog your memory to revisit those good times and laugh at those awkward or embarrassing moments. Enjoy who you were and who you are now. Open your eyes to a bigger picture and get a better perspective of women; whether it's yourself, your girlfriend, or just a friend. Look at them differently. Look beneath those breasts. You might have to lift them up a little to look . . . but take a closer look. You will be surprised and encouraged at what you find.

Learn to laugh at yourself. Be proud of yourself no matter what stage in life you are in. There is more to you than just boobs and your bra size doesn't define you. It might annoy you . . . but it doesn't define you.

Boob Job

I used to joke quite often about getting a boob job. I would say "if I ever had an extra $5,000 to spare, I would get a breast augmentation". It's a pretty common procedure these days and a lot of people have it done and they look better in my opinion.

No one talks about the risks of your appearance 20 years down the road. Picture this . . . a woman gets a boob job at age 40. Then 20 years pass. Now in her 60's she has the boobs of a 20 year old but her face shows the wrinkles of grandma time. How ridiculous!

Like I said, I used to joke about getting a boob job . . . until I met Joel, that is. Joel is a young man I worked with. He was 21 at the time and I was already in my 40's. Jokingly, I mentioned my desire to purchase a new set of boobs. Joel replied back with "fake boobs are such a turn off". ??!! I was shocked to hear that but was pleased to know at least one man on the planet felt that way.

So I started thinking . . . if Joel feels that way, surely, there has to be more men that feel the same way. So I am calling all men to stand up and let your voice be heard! Yell if from the rooftops if you must.

Now, realistically, we know there is a majority of men that do not share Joel's opinion. These men lose brain cells the minute a woman with a 36 DD bra size walks in the room. I, for one, want to be around these men in their golden years; when they have to face the cold hard fact that gravity does not affect women only. Oh yes men, gravity affects more than just boobs.

Now you change the title of this book to fit yourself if you like. They're just Boobs Get over it to They're just balls get over it.

Get what I'm saying guys? Come on gentlemen. That doesn't define your manhood anymore then it defines us as women. The way you treat people shows what kind of man you are; how you treat your wife and your children. How you live your life is what defines who you are. They really are just boobs! P.S. Thank you Joel!

Milking Time

It still amazes me that one of God's creations is the food supply for babies through our bodies. We all would agree that nursing a baby is the best way to go. It's best nutritionally and gives bonding time between baby and mommy.

I've heard women say it's such a wonderful experience and, it is. You would think nursing would be an easy thing to do since it's a natural process. That's not always the case, though. It doesn't make you a bad mother if you're not able to breast feed. Just no propping bottles please! Hold them babies!

I nursed my first baby but when my second child came along I wasn't able to. Sometimes women don't produce enough milk or, because of soreness they just give up. In my case, I was going through a very stressful time in my life and was not eating properly. So formula was the best choice then.

I was a young mother and although I did nurse my first baby, I was inexperienced on what to expect. No one prepared me for the changes that would take place when my milk came in. I had no idea my boobs would swell three times their normal size. I was embarrassed when I awoke up to soaked sheets because I had leaked everywhere.

The fact that I could become a human fountain at any given moment was something I think I should have been informed of ahead of time. I remember standing in the shower with milk just streaming down. I felt like a cow lined up for milking time at the local dairy farm.

Although all of this was a natural part of breastfeeding, I was embarrassed. I felt like a freak of nature. One time in particular, I remember I was in the bedroom nursing my daughter and my husband walked in. He saw my boobs had miraculously grown to giant size and he clearly liked what he saw. His only response was "WOW!" Of course my reply would be "Get out!" He didn't care why they were bigger, he just liked that they were bigger.

At that moment I did not feel attractive. I surely didn't feel like the picture on the cover of a parenting magazine; you know, the one that has a photo of a size six woman nursing he baby and everybody looks peaceful and picture perfect.

Those magazines need to show some truth. But then again, if it showed engorged breasts with sore, cracked nipples I am guessing they wouldn't sell as many copies.

Sarah Laughed

One of my favorite Bible stories is the one of Sarah and Abraham. Sarah and Abraham were very old and Sarah had given him no children. A whole chain of events occurred prior and you can read the entire story if you like. I am going to fast forward to the part that makes me smile.

Sarah and Abraham were past the age of reproduction. God came to Abraham and told him Sarah would conceive and have a baby. Abraham fell on his face and laughed. Abraham questioned in his heart. "Sarah is 90, how is this possible?"

Later in the story, it tells that Sarah was off to the side listening and she laughed out loud. The Lord tells Sarah "I heard you laugh. Is anything impossible to God?"

At first, Sarah denies laughing. God answered "You did laugh". The fact that Sarah laughed is so understandable, right?

It's interesting to me how that story is not so different from the way women look at themselves today. Youthfulness had left Sarah. The possibilities of having a child or being intimate at all were gone. The very thought of it made Sarah laugh.

I personally was never bothered by the fact that child bearing years were over. I had two children and was content in that stage of life. I do understand how some women feel differently though. Sarah never had any children before that, so she surely wanted them. I've heard women talk about their circumstances and they felt like less of a woman because they couldn't have more children. It doesn't make you less of a woman. It just makes you in a different place of life.

Whatever you situation, I want you to laugh at whatever life throws at you. I want you to be content with who you are.

Reading through Genesis, I couldn't find a scripture that said Sarah talked to her friends about her situation. It might be in there and I just couldn't find it. That story happened how many thousands of years ago? Still not so different than today.

We all need each other. We need to listen and encourage each other. We definitely need to laugh together. Trials and struggles don't' seem so bad when you have a friend that goes through it with you. Who knows. In another thousand years you might be the next story written for someone else to read.

My favorite verse; Genesis 21:16, Sarah said "God hath made me laugh, so all that hear will laugh with me".

Common Bond

Good friends are vital to your life because we really do have a common bond. We need each other for those happy times. It makes laughing funnier and it makes tragedies not seem so overwhelming when you have a friend beside you. Of course, everyone prefers happiness and carefree lives but the truth is bad days happen. There is strength in numbers.

The next few pages are not going to be comical. I am going to talk about the most tragic and devastating think I've ever had to observe. I think pretty much everyone has had to deal with cancer personally; either within your own immediate family or you know someone who has been affected by this disgusting disease. I imagine cancer is the worst thing a person can be forced to deal with. For a woman to hear the words breast cancer it becomes personal. It's offensive. God bless the courageous women and men who are dealt this struggle and choose to be warriors.

Modern Day Heroes

Let me share with you about two beautiful ladies I am blessed to call my friends, Barbara (Barbie) Morrison and Anne (Annie Bell) Stump. Both of these women have family members who were faced with cancer.

Barbie had two sisters diagnosed with cancer and sadly they both lost the fight but went on to be made whole in the presence of the Lord, Della Wood Murphy and Patty Wood Murphy. When

I say they lost the fight, they did exactly that. They fought.

They were strong and they were warriors. They were wives and mothers who left behind families who are still affected by their lives.

I knew these women personally. I spent time with them. I sat in their homes. I shared meals with them. These were two of the strongest women I had the benefit of knowing.

Annie's mother, Mrs. Nancy Stump, was diagnosed with breast cancer in 1982 and had to have a mastectomy. Annie and I work together and her parents would stop in periodically. Nancy is still a survivor today. Thank you God. She continues to be a faithful wife and an example to her family. She sacrificed a body part but her life is more than just the physical. I am still encouraged when I get to see her. She always has a smile on her face and has kept the faith through adversity. The strength of all these women is incredible. I could write pages of stories that Annie and Barb have shared with me.

Of course there were sad moments. It's an overwhelming attack, but through it, I heard stories of strength. I heard about the laughter in the middle of what they went through because of the way they handled it.

These women really got it. They understood that there is more to them and more in life than the physical.

They really are just boobs!

Badge of Courage

First of all, I applaud every woman for their courage and strength. This is no way intended to be insensitive or minimize what you endured.

If you lost your breasts to that vicious disease, I just want to tell you, you are beautiful! Your scars are a badge of courage. Your strength is encouragement to other women.

There is a scripture that says "if it offends thee, cut it off." Better to enter into heaven without that body part than not to be there with a whole body.

Maybe I am taking it out of context but I think it still applies. Cancer is offensive. It has taken people I love. It is the worst attack on mankind's existence. So better to enter into his kingdom without that body part because that is the place you will truly be transformed. You win!

Greatest Love Story Ever Told . . . Includes Boobs

The greatest love story I've ever read was the Song of Solomon. In my opinion, the Song of Solomon is the most descriptive story about a woman from her man's point of view. It describes her body in detail—even her boobs. That's right; boobs are mentioned in the Bible, confirming to me that the fascination with boobs has been happening for thousands of years.

43

Songs of Solomon 1:2 says, "Let him kiss me with the kisses of his mouth for thy love is better than wine." In Chapter 4, he is describing his bride: how lovely she is and the attraction between them. Verse 4:3, "Thy lips are like a thread of scarlet and they speech is comely. Thy temples are like a piece of pomegranate within they locks" Verse 4, "Thy neck is like a tower. Thy breasts are like two young roes that are twins which feed among the lilies."

Chapter 7:1-5, "How beautiful are thy feet. Thy joints of thy thighs are like jewels. Thy navel is like a round goblet . . . they belly is like wheat set about the lilies. Thy neck is a tower of ivory. Thine eyes like fish pools. Thine head upon thee is like carmel. How fair and pleasant art thou. Thy stature is like a palm tree and thy breasts to a cluster of grapes!"

Now that descriptive! It listed various body parts but did you notice that boobs were mentioned multiple times. Kind of makes me glad that I am a woman.

Yeah, Menopause!

At age 42, I went for a random check-up and was asked if there was a chance I could be pregnant. I laughed out loud and answered "that is impossible on so many levels". I had my tubes tied when I was in my 20's and am not currently having sex. Yeah, most likely, not pregnant. At my check-up, the doctor informed me that I had a problem. After an ultrasound, it was confirmed I had a cantaloupe sized tumor.

In 2006, I have a hysterectomy which threw me into menopause. People warned me about what happens to women during menopause. I heard all the horror stories about hot flashes and night sweats. I was already prepared for mood swings and yes, ladies admit it, we have mood swings. Although, I thought I was prepared for this upcoming event, no one bothered to mention the effects menopause has on boobs!

I was not prepared for the soreness and pain in my breasts and let's be honest—at age 40, gravity has started to take over. That's enough reality for anyone.

This time in life was probably the most challenging I'd have to admit. I personally wasn't depressed about not being able to have more children. I was past that part of my life and I was content. I surely didn't care if I had another monthly period ever again. What

I was concerned with was . . . I wanted my boobs back! You know the originals! Full and perky. It's not that anybody but me sees them lately anyway since I've been single for a long time. But I still wanted them back.

I've always wondered where certain words originated from. For example: Menopause? We all know what it really means but I think the truth is that it's code for other things. Men pause at finding us interesting or we pause at being interested in men.

I have chosen to use natural supplements to help with the effects of menopause and after trying different kinds, I finally found one that helps. You can get depressed just reading the labels on the bottles. They claim those pills eliminate water gain, reduce sleeplessness and hot flashes. No wonder we have mood swings! It goes without saying menopause is challenging but it's a change we have to accept. I've heard the word cycle used when referring to menopause and it is all part of the cycle in our lives. But I have found it to be true that it does not have to be a vicious cycle.

It's An Illusion

It's funny to me when someone asks me if I've lost weight when I haven't lost a pound or when they comment "you look thinner in that dress". Certain clothes are more flattering than others and for example black makes a person appear thinner. By the way did I mention my favorite color is black? In addition to that deceptive color of clothing, there is a nifty invention called the bra.

There are so many types that give an illusion to your shape. First there is the push up bra. That is pretty self-explanatory. The sports bra is meant to be more binding to prevent bouncing during exercise. There's also the minimizer bra. Something I clearly never had use for. Then there's my mom's favorite, the padded bra. I am pretty sure my mom's reason for recommending a padded bra is because it really does make your appearance in a blouse more attractive. It will also prevent anyone from noticing when you are cold. I choose not to wear a padded bra because it's false advertising. IT'S PADDED! IT'S AN ILLUSION! It hides the harsh reality of my true size. I don't want to mislead anyone, especially my future husband. Just picture it. I am dressed up looking more physically youthful than I really am. Black dress, control top pantyhose, and a padded bra. Mr. Right swoops in for that big moment of intimacy. My bra comes off and my boobs disappear!! I can only imagine the horror that hits him when he realizes what has happened. Disappointment is not the reaction I want to see at that moment.

The way I see it, no false pretenses. What you see is what you get . . . work with it.

Midlife Crisis—Or Not

Have you ever wondered why they call it a midlife crisis? Certain behaviors or a sudden change of behavior in a middle aged person gets labeled as a crisis.

When a man is supposedly having a midlife crisis, stereotypically, he starts changing his appearance. He may get a new hairstyle or purchase a totally different wardrobe. He starts shopping for a new car; perhaps a classic hot rod or just a sports car. He wants to get noticed or maybe just be reassured he is still attractive.

As a woman, I can only speak for myself. What I would relate to my midlife crisis is that my kids are grown and the grandkids are now consuming a big part of my time. I feel like I am losing myself to being a caregiver all over again. The crisis is not my family. I loved being a mother even though I was single and I love being a grandmother. It's just through the years I forgot how to love just being Tresa.

I am a great cook but I am not just a cook. I am the woman who wants to get dressed up and be taken out on a date to a nice restaurant. I am not just the woman who takes care of the kids and babies. I want to be that desirable lady that a man wants to make love to . . . just without making babies.

Isn't midlife supposed to be referring to the middle part of life? What age exactly is midlife? Is there a set time where your desire to be valued changes? Does it increase just because you are half way through life? If that were true than a man who dies at age 40 would have a midlife crisis at age 20.

Realistically thinking doesn't all men and women want to feel attractive to somebody? Don't all men and boys already want sporty cars? The material things do become more of an issue as men age but not because they are having this so called crisis but because after years of hard work he has gotten older and he really just wants to have tangible evidence that he was successful in life.

It doesn't seem right to compare midlife to crisis. Is it really a crisis or an awakening? For lack of a better word, it's destination. That's right, we have arrived and we are smarter. Of course we would like to stop the aging clock from ticking but as much as we try we can't stop time. So let's get off our butts and enjoy every minute.

I personally intend to mark things off my bucket list; like ride in another bike tour or run my first 5K. I want to see the Statue of Liberty and lay on the beaches of Fiji. The most exciting thing on my bucket list is to go bungee jumping. I will be fearless and sassy and before I jump I'll make sure to tell the little blonde Barbie doll next to me, "watch this, this is how us old girls do it!"

All of us mid-lifers do want material things, but not for greed purposes. We want things so we can relax and enjoy the next 25 years. Why? Because we earned it. I personally worked hard all my life and it's comforting to know that I have a few monetary things to leave my family when I am gone. That is if I don't spend it all . . . having fun.

Be a Rebel—Not Delusional

When we are young and we think we have the world at our fingertips, we so often take for granted our youth. We go through our 20's and even our 30's never giving thought to how the next decade will change us.

You wake up and realize 20 years flew by and we're not as vibrant as we use to be. Not only mentally have we changed. We look down to rediscover that change has ravished our bodies. The big question is . . . how will you embrace your transformation?

I heard a saying once that "youthfulness is wasted on the young." Makes sense doesn't it? I for one don't intend to grow old gracefully. I intend to rebel against it as much as possible. I want to encourage you to do the same.

Strive to maintain youthfulness but embrace the wisdom you've obtained through the years. Read more. Exercise more. Be smart about life but learn to laugh at things you can't control, like gravity.

You can lift weights seven days a week and you will look better I am sure. Yes it works. I am not saying you shouldn't be health conscious because you should. That's just common sense. Try to make the most of your activities. Take up walking but do it outside so you can see the flowers or talk to a person you've never met before. Go sledding with a six year old. You'll quickly be reminded of the reality of your age. Take a class at a local college. If you've never been on a train, hop on! What a fun way to see the states! Learn to play an instrument or take a dance class. Just do something! Step out of your comfort zone.

Whether you are concerned with gravity or not. Whether you are content with your body image or not. The main thing is health. Take care of yourself so you will be here an extra 20 years . . . but I am guessing a few chest presses at the gym can't hurt, right?

Fun Little Facts

- Breast Augmentation traces back to the 19th century. The earliest breast augmentation was recorded in 1895 and was performed by Dr. Vincez Czery after removing a tumor.
- Garments that were worn to restrain breasts date back to ancient Greece and were called breast bands.
- The bra replaced the corset in late 19th century.

- The first modern brassiere to receive a patent was invented in 1914 by Mary Phelps Jacob.
- In 1948 the first push up bra was introduced by Fredrick Mellinger who is the infamous Fredrick's of Hollywood. (This is my favorite fun fact because I've always known it had to be a man to come up with this.)
- Timi Jean Linsey from Texas, in 1962, was the guinea pig for a breast augmentation in the U.S.
- In 2008 archaeologists were working at the Landenberg Castle in Eastern Austria and discovered 2700 fragments of textile, among them were 4 bras.

Mark We Leave

We go through life but once and our mark on the world we leave behind.

What kind of mark will we leave and what evidence will they find?

Is the heart a happy place or one that's filled with grief?

Are the memories for others good or is it regrets that we leave?

Are the arms a place of safety for a tired friend to rest?

Is your conversation one of cursing or of one that is blessed?

Have you always done to others like you would have them do?

Or do you only speak kind words when they are first extended to you?

This world would be a better place if we all would keep in mind, we leave a trail behind us for someone else to find.

When we're dead and gone, what will others say?

Will they know we blessed them to provide a better way?

Make memories that you leave behind ones that people cherish.

For loving kindness and forgiveness are things that never perish.

Life is so uncertain and feelings are so frail.

Leave happy memories when you go—they mark an eternal trail.

T. Bowlin
2002

Acknowledgements

Thank you to everyone who contributed positive feedback while I worked on this,

To my daughter, Ashley, for encouraging me to keep writing. To my lifelong friend, Barb, thank you for being a sounding board for this book's content. (Man did we laugh a lot). To my kids, Ashley and Austin, the two most stubborn people I know, thank you for keeping me on my toes and making me laugh. You gave me memories that will last forever. Most of all, thank you for giving me the funniest grandkids on the planet; Madeline, Austin Michael, Benjamin, Allison, and Dakota . . . they remind me daily of what is important. To my mother for always being an example of what a lady should look like. To daddy—thank you for passing on your gift of humor. I miss you so much! Last but sure not least! Thank you most to Jesus Christ. I have no peace or joy unless you are surrounding me.